ADVANCE PRAISE FOR DOMINANT THOUGHTS

"Read this book if you want to do BIG things, read it and you'll trust your gut, take more action, and be inspired to fulfill your potential, GO!"

Tom Ferry, #1 Real Estate Coach and Speaker,
NY Times Bestselling Author

"A must read, the lessons and learnings in this story are timeless and priceless."

Glenn Sanford, CEO eXp World Holdings,
CEO SUCCESS Enterprises

DOMINANT THOUGHTS

Things Grow Where Our Minds Go

Chris Heller ▪ Greg S. Reid

Dominant Thoughts

Things Grow Where Our Minds Go

Chris Heller and Greg S. Reid

ISBN-13: 978-1-956503-71-5 print edition

ISBN-13: 978-1-956503-72-2 ebook edition

Waterside Productions

2055 Oxford Ave

Cardiff, CA 92007

www.waterside.com

For bulk orders, please visit

www.DominantThoughts.com

Printed in the United States of America

CONTENTS

1

THE BIG QUESTION

The transaction had been years in the works and months in the making, and now the day had finally arrived. The 350-million-dollar sale of John's business was completed earlier that morning, and with the ink still drying on the newly signed agreement, both buyer and seller had returned to the company's headquarters, where a less formal, but final, celebration would take place.

The boardroom was packed for the event, which represented a sendoff to John, the founder of the well-known local business empire he built from scratch, and a welcome to the excited new buyer, an ambitious entrepreneur who had impressive successes under his belt.

It would culminate in an open house, where all staff were welcome to drop in and meet the new proprietor.

The vice president who had served alongside John for the last decade took the floor. He opened his speech by thanking their founder for having the vision and ability to create a successful business that provided income and opportunities for so many in the community.

He then wished John well in his future endeavors, or what he referred to as his "semi-retirement."

Then, the VP turned the focus to the new owner and the executives who were coming on board with him.

"Let's give a warm welcome to the new owner of M.A.R. Enterprises, as we commit to working together to build on the success of this phenomenal company."

Standing off to the side, John joined in the applause. There was no sadness, no regrets. He was proud of the business and his accomplishments, and the staff had served him well. In hindsight, he had accomplished everything he had set out to do—and more.

It was time to let the business prosper under new ownership and vision, and it was time for John to explore other opportunities on a more personal level. There were things he wanted to do, and the sale of the business gave him the resources and time to expand beyond the reach of the company and into different areas.

If anything, he was excited to explore what was next on the horizon.

And just like that, 20 minutes later, the "official" ceremony was over. The press had concluded its photo shoot, with the last pose being the old and new regime shaking hands in solidarity. Out with the old ... in with the new.

People swarmed around the new owner, extending their congratulations and welcomes as they followed him out of the room like little ducklings, and suddenly John felt out of place.

His essence was no longer needed, and it shouldn't be. He'd said all of his goodbyes over the course of the last several weeks and thanked every employee in every department for their dedication and their efforts, letting them know that they were each a fundamental part of the success of the business. Today, he enjoyed seeing them take ownership of their efforts as they welcomed their new leader—they had moved on, and he suddenly realized that he should, too.

It was time.

Grabbing his backpack, John looked around the emptied room and smiled. As he quietly slipped out the door, he was confident that he was leaving his business and his employees in good hands.

"Sir! Sir!" a voice yelled as he was placing the last of his personal items in his car.

Looking up, John noticed a young man running toward him.

"Excuse me! I noticed that you left before you even had a piece of your cake, so I brought you one," he said, passing a plate toward him.

"Thank you. I appreciate it," John said, taking the plate. He nodded his head and cracked a smile before closing his still opened trunk.

"Umm, wait. Sir, can I ask you a question before you go?" the young man asked hesitantly.

"Of course," John replied. "How may I contribute?"

"Well, everyone is celebrating your success, and they should. It's awesome. But I'd like to know something more important."

"What's that?" the older man asked, dangling his keys.

"What is the ONE thing you would say that made you the success you are?"

"That's a good question," John pointed out. "Interestingly, no one has ever asked me that particular question before. They tend to look at the shiny objects, without realizing what it took to build them. I believe in taking action and rewarding people for it, so I commend you for asking. Tell me, what is your name, young man?"

"Nick, sir—my name is Nick. Not Nick Sir," he said, fumbling his words.

"Happy to meet you, Nick. I tell you what, if you really want to know the magic key to my success, here's my number. Call me tomorrow morning at 10:10 and let me know you're ready."

The next morning, John's phone rang. Reaching for it, he saw the time: 10:11 a.m.

"Hi, it's me, Nick—you told me to call you this morning. I'm ready."

"You're late," John replied and to Nick's surprise, John immediately hung up the phone.

Not sure what had happened, Nick decided to give it another try. He called back, but this time before hanging up a second time, John said, "I'll give you another chance. Call me tomorrow at 10:10 a.m."

The next day, Nick did as instructed. He called at 10:10 a.m.

"You're late," the man said, and once again, the line was abruptly disconnected.

Nick stared at the phone, wondering what was going on. Late? he thought, looking at the clock. He wasn't late—he was right on time.

But not one to give up, Nick tried one more time. On the third day, he called promptly at 10:05 a.m.

"I'm ready," were the only words he spoke this time.

"Yes, the fact that you took this action and didn't give up tells me that you just might be," John confirmed. "If you want to know how I created my success, meet me at the Gold Shea restaurant at noon this Thursday. But don't come empty handed. I want you to bring something with you."

"What's that?" Nick asked, eager to comply with whatever was asked of him.

"Bring me a rabbit and a 20-dollar gift card."

"A *what?*" Nick asked, not sure if he'd heard him correctly.

"You heard me. Don't forget to bring them, and be on time," John said, then gently hung up the phone before Nick could ask another question.

Nick spent the better part of the rest of the day searching for the items. The gift card was easy, and he went straight to the mall to pick one up.

But a rabbit? That was something altogether different—if he had, indeed, even heard the man right. After all, why would anyone ask for a rabbit?

After a great deal of thought, he ruled out a live animal—he didn't even know where to find one. Besides, how would he transport it … and a restaurant probably wouldn't welcome one in their doors if he could find one.

Perusing several stores, he realized that there was no shortage of stuffed animals—they came in every size and color. He mulled over cute pink bunnies and larger white rabbits with fluffy cotton tails. But none of them appealed to him, so he finally settled on a brown ceramic version that he found hiding on a back shelf at the local thrift store.

It was nothing more than a trinket, but in his mind, it was more fitting than a child's toy.

Even though he was ten minutes early, when Nick arrived at the restaurant, he found that John was already there.

"Here you go," he said, sliding into the opposite side of the booth, while handing over the gift card and the small brown figurine. "Can I ask you, sir, what this is all about? I mean, why did you want me to bring a gift card and a rabbit, of all things?"

John smiled as he looked over the items, then said, "First, let me say that you followed instructions very well. Next, let me answer your question. I asked you to bring these things with you today because I wanted to know that you are ready to do whatever I ask, no matter how seemingly trivial or strange it may sound, because sometimes that's what it takes to be successful. From experience, I've found that most people are in their comfort zone, and that's where they like to stay. They're afraid of stepping out and doing something out of their norm, even if it will lend to their success. The fact that you were willing to comply with my request tells me that you are willing to do what others aren't so you can achieve what others haven't."

"Really? That's what this was all about?" Nick replied.

"Yes. You see, most people do want to be successful, but most people aren't willing to go out of their way and take action, applying the principles they learn. Let's just say this was an exercise to see where your thoughts lie. I needed to know if you really want to know the keys to my success and if you're ready to do whatever it takes to make it happen."

"But why the card? Why a rabbit?" Nick couldn't hide the curiosity in his voice.

"You will see. More important, understand this: Whatever you seek, whatever you are looking for is also seeking you in return. Pop quiz: Do you believe in the law of attraction and that our thoughts become things?"

The boy stuttered a bit in his reply. "I guess so, yeah."

"Ehhhhhhhh," the man blurted, sounding like the buzzer at the end of a game show.

"Well, let me reword that question. Did you ever have a great idea that came to you in the shower or something and yet never did anything about it?"

The young man nodded yes.

"Only to see as time goes by that your same idea came to life because someone else created it before you?"

"Boy, have I," the lunch guest whispered under his breath.

"The fact is, our thoughts DO become things by the **progress** we make toward them, and it's that ACTION in the law of attrACTION that makes our dreams come true. Yes, you have to think it, yes, you have to feel it, and yes, ultimately you have to do it!"

Nick grabbed the first thing he could find and jotted the note down, saying, "Wow, that's a good one."

"Love that! There you go—you did it! You took action by writing that down, and that deserves another meeting. Same place, same time next week?" the gentleman suggested.

"Absolutely," the student eagerly agreed. "What do I have to bring next time? A frog? A dinosaur?" he laughed.

"Great question," the man remarked with a smile. "Just come with a notepad next time so you don't have to jot things down on the kids' menu."

As the two headed toward the door to exit, Nick watched his host slip a $100 bill into the busboy's hand and handed him the two items the young man had brought in. As he whispered something in his ear, the busboy's eyes lit up.

"What was that about?" the young man asked.

"His family lost all their household items in a house fire last month, and I knew his son could use the gift card, and his mother would appreciate the statue. It is a symbol of good luck in many cultures. Good job, kid—you made someone's day today."

Walking to their cars, the two shook hands, which, although they didn't know it at the time, would become a bond that would last a lifetime.

2

SHOW UP

The next week, Nick arrived even earlier than he had the week before, hoping that this time, he would arrive before John. But to his surprise, the older gentleman was already seated at the table and had already polished off half of a cup of coffee.

This guy brings a whole new meaning to the word "punctual," he thought. *Next time, I'm going to beat him at his game. I'll turn the tables and be waiting for him!*

"Good afternoon," greeted the man. "I see you remembered to bring a notepad. Being prepared is an admirable quality."

"Thanks, but to be honest, you did tell me to bring a notepad, so I guess I can't take credit for it," the young man admitted.

"Well then, you've followed instructions quite well. Let's leave it at that."

After their server took their lunch order, John wasted no time.

"Nick, you indicated that you want to know how I became successful. What did I do? How did I do it? I'm willing to share that with you. But with my advice and counsel comes responsibility. Are you prepared to assume that responsibility?"

"What do you mean by responsibility?"

"Knowledge is a very valuable possession, young man. If I pass my knowledge on to you, it will be worthless unless you use it and share it. By passing it on to you, I expect you to make sure it retains and even increases in value. Can I trust you to do that?"

Thinking that this sounded like being entrusted with top-secret information, Nick agreed.

"Yes, sir. I won't let you down. Tell me, is this something that nobody else knows?" There was a sense of mystery, even secrecy in his voice.

"I cannot say that. As a matter of fact, much of what you will learn in our time together is decades, even centuries, old. They were passed on to me through books, teachers, and mentors. However, I will also teach you some things that I've learned on my own. I've found that experience and challenges can be phenomenal teachers. Regardless, they have been instrumental in my success."

"Wow!" Nick exclaimed, then looking at the notepad next to his plate, he added, "But I think I'm going to need a bigger notebook."

"I wouldn't worry about that today. It's far too much to share in one day, and even if I could, it would be too much to comprehend in one sitting."

"Whew! So when do we get started?" the young man asked eagerly.

"I like to say that there's no time like the present," John replied.

Grabbing his pen, Nick opened his notepad and informed the gentleman across the table that he was ready.

"So what's the first thing I need to know?"

"Well, it's something you've already done," the man smiled.

"What's that?"

"Show up. You can never be successful at anything if you don't show up. Think about it—you can't win a race if you don't run it, can you?"

"No," Nick laughed.

"Right. It's also true that you can't sit back and not put any effort into your life and expect to have phenomenal results. I can tell you that you have a better chance at becoming wealthy if you show up in everything you do. If you have a job, show up. But don't just go to work—go to work on time every single day, ready to learn and do whatever it takes. If you own a business, you absolutely have to show up. Your business is your responsibility. Nobody else is going to do it for you. *You* have to be present, and you have to be prepared, no matter how much hard work it takes."

"Okay," the young man muttered as he furiously jotted down the man's words.

"But there's more to it. I said you have to show up and be present, and that means that you have to be focused on the task at hand. If you're physically there but your mind is preoccupied with something else, you haven't shown up at all, have you?"

"No, I guess not," the young man agreed.

"Of course, not. And that's one of the biggest problems I've seen. People think that showing up is enough. As long as they're there, they've done their part. But that falls far short of what it takes to build a legacy of success. When I say you need to show up, I mean you have to be all in, giving your full time and attention to your duties, your responsibilities, and your business. When I'm at work, I'm working. I'm not messing around on the Internet, checking my phone, or doing as little as possible to pass the time until quitting time. It's also true that when I'm at play, I'm playing. When I'm on the tennis court or dining at a restaurant with my wife, I'm not checking my email or trying to drum up sales. I'm present and attentive to the moment. If I weren't, I have no doubt that I'd lose that tennis match, and you can bet my wife would know that my time and attention weren't where they should be," he chuckled.

"This is good stuff, and it doesn't sound all that hard!" the young lad exclaimed.

"Well, I guess this is a good time for a word of caution," the man stated.

"What's that?"

"It isn't always easy to show up, Nick. There will be times when showing up might be the last thing you want to do."

"Like when?"

"On days when you have to tell your staff that budget cuts are necessary—that's never easy, and nobody ever wants to do it. But it has to be done. There will be things that you don't want to do, or even dread doing, but that's when you're being put to the test. I can attest to the fact that it's not always easy to show up. So can Andy."

"Who's Andy?"

"Andy is our busboy—remember that I told you that his family lost everything in a house fire? Well, do you know that Andy actually came to work the day after the fire? Nobody expected him to, not by a long shot, but he walked through that door on time and ready to work."

"You're kidding!" Nick was amazed.

"Let me ask you, do you really have what it takes to show up, no matter what? On good days and bad days? The answer to that question is critical because it is what ultimately will separate those who become successful and those who can't seem to break through the barrier that's holding them back."

"Did you have those kinds of days?" Nick asked, so intent he couldn't hide the curiosity in his voice.

"You bet I did. More than I'd like to admit. But that was in the beginning. You see, I found that the more I showed up and was present in every way, the less often I had to worry about those kinds of days."

The mentor smiled as he watched the pearl of wisdom sink in.

"You're off to a good start, son. When I told you to call me, you showed up—a little late, yes, but you caught on," he smiled. "And when I told you to meet me here, you showed up and did what I asked of you. If you are willing to continue with that same level of commitment, let's meet again next week."

"You bet I can! I'm going to show up and be present. You can count on that! So is there anything I need to do before then?"

"Keep what we talked about today in the front of your mind. No matter what you're doing, make a conscious effort to show up—not just with your body, but with your mind. Give whatever you do your all. By that, I mean don't do anything halfway or half-heartedly. If you can do that all week long, you'll begin to see a difference, not just in your results, but in *you.* You see, you're not only changing your habits, but you're changing your thoughts. One of the most important things you'll learn in our time together is that success isn't all about knowledge or education—it's about the thoughts you choose to prioritize and implement in your life. I call those dominant thoughts. If you want to pursue success, it starts in your mind ... but if you don't religiously show up for the pursuit, you'll always be chasing something that's out of your reach."

3

DON'T LISTEN TO YOUR WANTS AND DON'T WANTS

For the next week, Nick attempted to show up in everything he did. As an entry-level salesperson in his first job out of college, he wasn't immune to frustration. Knowing he had to put in his time before he could climb the ladder was a reality that tested his patience. There were times when he thought he couldn't sit through yet another sales meeting and hearing the same strategies and benchmarks being repeated again and again.

As he tried to "show up" at the weekly meeting, these feelings were intensified.

I want to show up ... but I don't want to endure this for another hour. My time would be put to better use contacting potential clients ... nothing happens when nothing gets done, he thought.

As soon as the thought crossed his mind, he became conscious of it. *Focus,* he told himself. *Listen, learn, show up.*

And he did. It took a conscious effort to be fully present, during that meeting and throughout the week. But as he became more and more aware of his tendency to drift anywhere but there, he increased his ability to prevent the desire and any wandering thoughts.

Then, it occurred to him to be more present in his conversations. When he was on the phone, whether setting up an appointment or delivering a sales pitch, he gave all of his attention to the person on the other end of the conversation.

And to his surprise, he found it made a difference. He became more engaged, both in meetings and in conversations. He became more present. He was doing exactly what John suggested--he was showing up.

And it showed.

Remembering the promise he'd made to himself, he showed up to the Gold Shea 20 minutes early the next week. Seeing John across the room, he sighed. Once again, his new mentor was a step ahead of him.

After placing their lunch orders, Nick excitedly brought John up to date, telling him that he had made an intentional effort to show up at work and admitting that he was surprised, but excited, to see that it made a difference.

"I don't know if other people noticed it, but *I* did ... I felt like I wasn't just going through the motions, like I had a purpose," he said.

"Very good—I'm glad to hear it. And you do have a purpose, Nick. My guess is that you just don't know what it is, not yet, anyway," the older man surmised. "Let's see if I can help you in that area. Tell me about your goals. Have you set any? Did you set goals in college?

"Sure, I did. One was to graduate, and I did that," Nick grinned.

"Okay. Were there any goals you didn't achieve?" the mentor inquired.

A brief pause prefaced his answer.

"Yes, I guess there were some."

"Like what?" John prodded, wishing that the young man across the table would be more forthcoming in his responses.

"Well, there were a lot of things I wanted to do. When I got my acceptance letter, I had big dreams--I thought I'd be a big man on campus. You know, I'd be super popular ... and smart. I'd kick college's butt and show it who was boss. I wanted to join the best fraternity and maybe even be president of it. I guess it was the typical stuff, full of independence, success, friends, and fun. Oh, and girls," he grinned.

"Ahhh, yes, typical college goals. I hear them often from college students. Tell me, which of those goals did you accomplish? Be truthful here, it's important that you're honest, especially with yourself," the man cautioned.

A faraway look entered Nick's eyes as he quickly reflected on those four years of his life.

"I guess it's fair to say I gained some independence. And I did join a fraternity, but it wasn't the best by far. Oh, and I managed to make some friends, and I have to confess that I did have a lot of fun!"

"Fair enough. Now, which goals didn't you accomplish during those formative educational years?"

Nick's demeanor changed, and John thought he looked a bit sheepish as he spoke.

"I was never really popular or the big guy on campus. And I didn't make the dean's list or anything. I guess I could've done better, but ..."

"But what?" John asked, noting a hesitation.

"I'm not sure. Maybe I didn't apply myself like I could have," Nick admitted.

"In other words, you didn't show up?" the man asked, raising his eyebrows as he waited for verification.

"You're probably right. I never thought of it that way," he replied.

"I believe it might be safe to presume that those things you wanted weren't dominant in your mind, at least not compared to the many other things you might have wanted. Nick, is it possible that your wants and don't wants both got in your way?"

Looking at his mentor, Nick shook his head in confusion.

"I don't understand, sir. What do you mean, my wants and don't wants?"

"Hmmm, think of something you should have done, but didn't. The question is why didn't you?"

"Ummm, probably because I didn't want to," Nick answered, half guessing and half admitting.

"You're probably right. You fell into the trap of I don't want ... You tell yourself that you don't want to do something today, so you put it off. You don't want to put in extra effort, so you don't try. You don't want to give up a night hanging out with the guys, so you didn't put in that extra time you needed to research your term paper. Do you get the picture?"

"Yes, I think I do," Nick answered. "I'll admit I've been guilty of those things a time or two."

"I like your honesty."

"Thank you. But you said my don't wants and my wants. What about what I *want?"*

"Those can get in your way, too," the man stated.

"How so?"

"There are things we want that can stop us or get in the way of what we really want. For example, you know you should do something, but you want to hang out with your friends instead. Or there's a report or quota you really need to be working on—it's been nagging at you, but you really want to put it off. So you check social media, text a few friends, anything other than what you need to do or should do. Does that sound familiar?"

"Okay, guilty as charged. But in my defense, reports and sales quotas aren't very exciting," Nick replied.

"Not when they're not favorable ... but I assure you, when they are, they can be quite exciting, like hitting a home run," John countered.

"Oh, I see where you're going. So let me guess, I need to do what I don't want to do, and I need to stop doing what I want to do?" he asked.

The gentleman chuckled.

"That's one way of putting it. But remember showing up? How if you really show up, you can do one thing and get it done, and still have time to fully show up for the other things, as well? It's not either / or, all work and no play. It's about focus, commitment, and intentional effort. Nick, what I really want you to do is to set a goal. Find something you want, something you really want, and take steps to get it, without letting fleeting or passing wants and don't wants get in your way," his mentor explained. "Do you have such a goal?"

"Well, I want to buy a new car ... and a house ... and I want a promotion. I want to be my own boss. I want to be a millionaire!" he rattled them off as his desires entered his head.

"Whoa! Let's focus on one at a time. Pick one of those things--something you should be able to achieve if you really commit to it."

"Hmmm, okay. How about a car? I want to buy a new car," Nick replied with confidence.

"Okay, did you bring your notebook?" John asked.

"You bet!" Nick pulled it from his pocket.

"Write your goal down then. Between now and the next time we talk, I want you to figure out which car, the cost, when you want to buy it, and, based on your commissions, exactly how many sales you need to make to save enough to buy it. Your goals must be specific, and they must be measurable," the older man advised.

"Okay," Nick said, penning his goal in his notepad, taking a few moments to add the tip about wants and don't wants in the margin.

"John, can I ask you a question?"

"Sure, that is what I am here for."

"Someday are you going to tell me the *real* secret to your success, how you became the owner of a multi-million-dollar company? I mean, I'm learning things, but I was hoping you'd give me the *real* secret, the one nobody else knows."

"I am, son. And there is no one secret, no single tip or strategy to success—unless you count one specific thing," he mused.

"What's that?" Nick's head perked up, waiting in anticipation.

"Your thoughts, Nick. Your thoughts are the single most important factor in your results. They always have been, and they always will be. The more you control your thoughts and steer them in the direction you want them to go, the more they will work for you. The thoughts that dominate your actions and beliefs are those that will determine your results. Now, go get started. Your new car is waiting," he smiled.

That night, Nick set his alarm to go off an hour earlier than normal. He had every intention of getting to work early and putting in the work to get the results he wanted.

When the alarm rang, though, the shrill rudely pulled him out of a sound sleep. Moaning, he turned over and slapped the snooze button. *Getting up is the last thing I want to do,* he thought.

And that thought made him sit straight up. *Do what I don't want ... don't do what I want.*

Like every other day, he really wanted to sleep in a little longer. Unlike any other day, though, Nick swung his legs out of the bed and his feet hit the floor.

4

DISCIPLINE

For Nick, the most difficult part of having a goal and attempting to achieve it was staying committed to it. It wasn't until he had John to hold him accountable that he realized just how easy it was to put off taking action toward his goal of buying a new car. He caught himself thinking, *I have all day, I can do that later, that won't take too long—I'll be able to take care of it after I finish everything else,* and one old standby: *That's going to take too long—I don't even want to think about it.*

However, setting the goal was easy. He'd always known what kind of car he wanted. While the rest of the guys all pined for a fast, sleek sports car that turned heads as it zoomed down the freeway, Nick had always wanted an off-road vehicle, a tough and rugged four by four that could handle any terrain, from mountains to sand dunes. Now, that was the car of his dreams!

He could see it already—all shiny and black, fresh off the lot. He could even see the sticker price and all the extras added to the invoice, which was more than he'd ever paid for anything in his life. Was it worth it? John told him it had to be—if he didn't really want it enough to work for it, he'd never do what he had to do to reach his goal. In other words, it would go down as nothing more than a wish—one that ended with "tomorrow never comes."

The one thing Nick attempted to do was to make sure he focused on what he wanted in his car, avoiding any mention of what he didn't want. And he found it was helpful … focusing on what he didn't want would be nothing more than a distraction that would take his eyes off his goal.

As he promised he would, Nick sent John an email, stating his goal very specifically. His mentor challenged him to break it down into steps and give each step a deadline. How much do you need to save in six months to make this happen, Nick? What do you need to do today, tomorrow, next week to get to that milestone?

At first, Nick found the process to be fun … until it wasn't.

John noticed it, too. Initially, Nick reported his progress to his mentor frequently, and with a sense of pride. Then the emails came less frequently. Every week turned into every 10 days, then every two weeks. It was then that John knew that he needed to intercede.

Rather than their usual restaurant, John sent the young man an address with a note that simply said, "Meet me here at 10:00 a.m. Saturday. Don't be late."

At precisely 9:55 a.m., when Nick pulled into the car dealership, he spotted his mentor leaning against the rear bumper of an SUV.

He can't possibly think I can afford this yet, can he? Nick thought.

"Hey," he said after shaking John's hand. "Why are we here? You do know that I'm in no position to buy a car just yet, don't you?"

"I most certainly do know that," John affirmed. "And judging by my observations, you might not ever be in that position. Am I right?"

"What? No! Believe me, it's going to happen. I assure you of that. I just don't know when. It's going to take a lot of time to save enough for a decent down payment, and …"

At that moment, the two were approached by a salesman.

"Good morning! How can I help you? If you see anything you like, I'll be happy to grab the keys and you can go for a test ride," he offered in an upbeat voice.

"Um," Nick looked toward John, unsure how to respond.

"Thank you, but we are not here to purchase a vehicle today," John told the salesman.

"Oh? Why are you here?" the salesman asked, confused.

"We are here today to discover what it really takes to purchase a vehicle. If it's okay, I'd like to take this young man on a stroll through your lot this morning. In appreciation, I will keep your business card on hand and make sure we call on you when he is in the market for a new vehicle," John answered.

As the two men walked away, Nick noticed how vastly different they were. The salesman might have thought they were father and son, or perhaps grandfather and grandson. Apart from their ages, they were other vast differences. Nick was dressed in his usual weekend attire—jeans, a t-shirt, and a pair of well-loved athletic shoes. On the other hand, John wore immaculate leather loafers, creased slacks that looked like they came right off the sales rack that morning, and a shirt with a crisp white collar.

"I thought you were retired. Do you always dress like you're ready to go to the office?" he asked his mentor.

"I suppose I do," was the short answer.

"Why? I mean, you don't *have* to," explained Nick.

"Perhaps it is a habit after doing so every day for decades. But I believe it is more out of discipline," the older man said.

"Discipline?"

"Yes, discipline—one of the things I wanted to talk to you about today. Before I do, Nick, I want to point out that I've noticed you're not making the progress you initially were making toward your goal. Is there a problem?"

"Not really a problem. It's just that—well, it's hard. It's going to take a lot of work for me to make that kind of money, and realistically, it's going to take longer than I thought," Nick admitted.

"Ah, yes, work—the age-old dreaded four-letter word. I'm no stranger to it but am often perplexed by how many people actually let it get in the way of what they want—especially since it is often the one thing that will bring them the things they really want," John replied.

"Let me tell you a story, young man, and it all goes back to discipline. What is it, really? To me, discipline is a muscle to be developed, much like any other muscle needs to be trained and built up over time. As such, it has muscle memory, and through the habit of repetition, it can be developed in a strong fashion. Early on, when I was still green behind the ears, I knew the key to my success was grounded in productivity. The key was in following my schedule, which included doing all the activities I had to do in order to maximize my productivity. Did it take work? Sure it did—lots of work. Was it always fun? Of course not! Sometimes it was downright hard, and I had to push myself to do the next thing and then the next.

"Along the way, Nick, I discovered a strategy to help me push through my own self-imposed obstacles."

"What was it?"

"To develop the habit of discipline in following my schedule, I decided to do the hardest thing I could think of first, knowing if I mastered that, all else would be easier. Naturally a night person, I decided to start waking up at 4:30 a.m. every morning—not some mornings or most mornings, but every single morning. What I found was that, over time, it got easier and easier to get up at that time every day. Eventually, it became a habit, just like discipline. Yes, discipline is a habit, and just like muscles, you can strengthen it and build on it," John advised.

"Okay, I'm just not sure how to get started," admitted the young man.

"Finding small things to conquer with discipline helps build those muscles. For instance, you can take a different route every morning to the office each day, or something else that gets you out of your comfort zone. You have to get out of your current habits so you can replace them with habits that serve you better. Here's something small that exemplifies this principle. Most of us wear our watch or Fitbit on the same wrist all the time, right?"

"Right," Nick answered, looking down at the Fitbit wrapped around his left wrist.

"Try wearing it on the opposite wrist for two weeks to get beyond the awkward, uncomfortable feelings. Sure, it will feel strange at first. I bet you don't even notice that you're wearing it most of the time right now, but I assure you that when you switch it to the opposite hand, you'll notice it. But you'll notice it less and less as time goes on and it becomes more comfortable, more the norm. You might even have to remind yourself not to put it on your left wrist every morning for a week or so, but by the end of the two weeks, you won't even think about it anymore. You've disciplined yourself to do it. Are you following, Nick?" asked John.

"I think so. I'm not making any progress because I'm not doing anything differently. I have to break my old habits, get out of my comfort zone, and do what it takes, and that means I need discipline. Does that sum it up?" he smiled.

"Yes, it does—quite well, actually. You see, it's not just about how you spend your time; this applies to so much more. It's about everything. You need discipline in all areas of your life. The more disciplined you are with your time, the more time you will have. The more disciplined you are with money, the more money you'll have. The more disciplined you are with your diet and exercise, the better health and more energy you'll have," the older man said.

"And the more disciplined I am with all those things, the more progress I'll make!" Nick added.

"They do compound on each other if you have the discipline to do what you have to do to get what you want," agreed John.

"Even if it's hard? Even if it's uncomfortable?" Nick added.

"Especially if it's hard. But if you work that muscle long enough, it will become so strong that it won't seem hard anymore. It'll just be a habit—but this is one habit that will bring you what you want," said John.

"Like that car," Nick said, pointing to a shiny black, fully loaded SUV at the end of the front row of the lot.

"If you've got the discipline to make it happen, yes," smiled John. "And might I remind you that discipline can only become a habit if you stay on top of it. Ingrain the need for discipline in your mind and make it one of your most dominant thoughts, so it doesn't fall into the wayside. If you slack off, you will most definitely resort to your old, unproductive habits."

Nick returned his mentor's smile, and in response, he reached down to his left wrist, unbuckled his Fitbit and moved it ever so deliberately to his right wrist.

"I guess there's no time like the present. Let the muscle building begin!" he announced.

5

DON'T WORRY ABOUT WHAT OTHERS THINK

Building that muscle wasn't easy at first. Nick had to consciously think about it, and he quickly discovered that when he didn't keep it top of mind, it was easy to put it off or, even worse, forget about it altogether. But just as John had told him, the more he did it, the more natural it became. It wasn't long before he realized that it wasn't such an effort, after all. One day, it occurred to him that he didn't even have to think about it at all, because just like the band that now rested around his right wrist, it had become routine.

With his newfound discipline, he found that he was making progress toward his goal—well, actually, goals. Nick now had multiple goals set to propel him toward his larger goal, and he had discovered the advantages of looking at numerous ways to make it happen. For instance, not only was he putting money aside for a down payment on the car of his dreams, but he had also invested some money, knowing that a higher interest rate could give him a better return and help him reach his goal even faster.

The fact that he was making progress brought him a sense of satisfaction. And he applied that same drive and determination toward his job, often staying a little later or making an effort to arrive a bit earlier. As expected, people started to notice.

"Hey, Nick, what's up? You trying to make the rest of us look bad?" one of his coworkers chided.

Knowing that his coworker was just giving him a hard time, Nick laughed the comment off. It was just some friendly ribbing from one guy to another, that's all.

But a couple weeks later, the same coworker actually criticized him, saying he was trying too hard. Then later that week, when the members of their team made an impromptu decision to order lunch and have it delivered, the coworker called Nick out for opting out.

"I already brought my lunch today, so no thanks," Nick said.

"So what? Live a little—it's just lunch. It's not like it's going to break the bank," his coworker retorted.

"That's alright, but thanks for asking. I'm good," Nick replied.

But the encounters left him feeling uneasy. He and his coworkers had never had issues before, and they certainly hadn't criticized each other, even in jest. For some reason, things felt different, and he couldn't put his finger on the reason.

It wasn't until the female member of their team was given a special project that he really felt personally slighted, though. For some reason, their supervisor had singled her out and handed her a project that Nick really would have liked to have been given. It would have provided him an opportunity to show his supervisor that he was committed and capable, especially now that John had taught him a few things about being disciplined and proving he was worthy of consideration.

The next time he met with John, he shared his feelings.

"Ah, yes. Nick, you have to expect such things in a competitive world—especially when you're growing. You see, some people are comfortable when they're among like-minded people. Your coworker who thinks you're trying too hard—well, he's noticing that you've changed. Did it occur to you that perhaps he feels that your improved work ethic makes him look bad?"

"No, but you might have a point," the younger man replied.

"Oh, I know I do. And when he puts you down or points something out in front of others, it's likely that he's doing it because he knows you look better than him … so, what does he do? He turns the tables, so *you're* the one who doesn't look good."

"You might be onto something," Nick said. "So what do I do about it?"

"Nothing."

"Nothing? I'm supposed to just stand there and do nothing?"

"That's right. Your actions speak louder than your words in such circumstances. If you say something, you're playing right into his game. If you want my advice, I say the one thing you should do is stop worrying about what he, or anyone else, thinks of you. The only person you have to worry about is the person in the mirror. So focus on yourself—not them."

"You really think that will work?"

"I know it will. Sure, you might notice that your relationship with this individual becomes more distant, but from what you've told me, I think it already has. Your job is to worry about your job, not his opinion. That's the only thing you can control. It never helps to worry about what other people think, son. That will only hold you back."

"So I'm making too big of a deal out of it?" asked Nick.

"No, but you need to recognize that not everyone will be in your corner as you grow. And that's alright. Your job isn't to get their approval. I learned that way back when I first started making cold calls. The people around me absolutely hated making cold calls because they were worried about what people would think of them. They didn't know how the recipient would receive their call, and some of them took rejection very personally. But because I didn't focus on what others thought of me, things like making cold calls were not traumatic for me, like it was for them. I wasn't worried about what the prospect thought of me, so their opinion wasn't a dominant thought in my mind, and I learned long ago that the thoughts that dominate always determine every outcome."

"Hmm, so it's safe to say that you had thick skin?"

"Perhaps. But I like to think that I knew what I could and could not control. I couldn't control another person's reaction or opinion. I could only control my response to it. When you are worried about what others think of you, you tend to hold back. You play not to lose, or stay in a safe zone, versus going all out. In other words, you don't take a risk because you're afraid of what somebody else might say or think. When that happens, you can't win. You lose the reward," John explained.

"That's a good point. I'll give it a try and see how it works out," Nick commented.

"Good! I'd like to give you a piece of advice, though. Just as it was when you started the process of becoming disciplined, it's going to take a conscious effort at first. Here's what I recommend you do: whenever you notice that you're worried about what someone else might think or what somebody else's opinion is, redirect your focus. Take your attention totally off of that worry and put it toward something productive. When you do, you're going to notice something," the mentor offered.

"What's that?"

"That it is difficult to focus on two things at once, so you are either focusing on what someone might be thinking or you are focusing on what you need to do and doing your very best. I didn't compare myself to others; instead, I focused on the person in the mirror. I truly felt that the only person I had to compete with to be the best was myself—which brings me to the second situation you posed earlier, that another coworker was awarded a special project."

"Yes, that's entirely different, and I was going to ask what your thoughts about that are ..."

"My thoughts are much along the same line. Don't worry about anyone else. Like a sprinter running a race, if he or she is looking over their shoulder or to the left or right to see what the other runners are doing or where they are, they inevitably get passed. Worrying about whether you're keeping pace or whether someone else is going to pass you up will only slow you down. The reason, again, is that you can't focus on doing your best and what another person is doing, all at the same time. Something has to give, and it's usually your performance. When I was aspiring to reach the next level, I operated with blinders on. I only focused on the person in the mirror and intentionally avoided trying to keep up with or even give a thought as to what the next guy was doing. I knew any time or energy focused on someone else would only slow me down."

"Now that makes sense! I ran track in high school and college, so I can relate! Not only does it slow you down, but you can run off course or worse, stumble and fall!" Nick said.

"You sure can. But let me offer one more possibility—when you're worried about what someone else is doing, and wondering if they're doing something you're not, isn't it possible that it's because you don't have confidence in your ability? Maybe you're afraid someone is doing something better than you, and you need to play catch up so they don't pass you up or get too far ahead? What does that say to you, Nick?"

"I'm not sure," he admitted.

"Let me put it like this. Leaders always look ahead while they're leading their team to success. Those who look to others all the time aren't leaders, Nick. They're followers. Now, you can emulate your coworker and try to do what she does so you can be the next one to get that coveted special project. Or you can stop worrying about what she's doing and take the initiative and do something special on your own. That's what a leader does," said John.

"You are *sooo* right! I feel so much better. John, I'm not going to worry about them—the only person I have to worry about is me!"

"That's a decision that merits my approval," John said. "And remember, when you asked me how I became successful, I was a leader. That's what I do … and that's what you'll do one day, too."

6

DON'T BE ATTACHED TO THE OUTCOME

It was a Saturday morning, and the country club was the setting for one of Nick's biggest lessons. John had invited him to play a round of golf, and although Nick forewarned him that he was an amateur at best, he accepted the invitation. A less formal social outing with his mentor sounded like a nice change of pace.

"Great," John said. "I'm looking forward to it. Be there at 8:00 a.m. sharp. We don't want to miss our tee time."

That morning, Nick pulled into the parking lot of the scenic country club at precisely 7:46 a.m., nearly 15 minutes early. He had learned that being on time didn't impress John—oh, no, John expected more. He meant to be ready and prepared *before* 8:00.

Pleased with himself, he got out of his car and opened his trunk to pull out his secondhand set of clubs. When he turned around, John was standing behind him with his clubs already loaded on a golf cart.

With a silent chuckle, Nick shook his head, wondering how the guy did it. No matter how hard Nick tried, John always arrived before he did. Somehow, he managed to be a step ahead of him all the time.

One of these days, I'm going to beat him at his game, Nick thought to himself. But it didn't look like it was going to be today.

"Good morning!" John greeted him. "Perfect day for a round of golf, isn't it?"

"It sure is. Let's just hope I don't slow you down too much."

"Think positively, Nick. There is more to golf than skill. The mental game is a big part of the sport," John advised.

They made it through the front nine and half of the back nine before the conversation shifted toward work.

"Hey, Nick, when is your interview?" John asked.

A promotional opportunity had come up, and Nick had been encouraged to apply for it by both his supervisor and John. Initially, Nick believed that the interviews were just a formality—that they already knew who they wanted to fill the position—his coworker, the one who had been given the special project that he had wanted. However, when his supervisor commented on the fact that they'd noticed a marked improvement in his performance, as well as an increase in his sales numbers, he thought maybe, just maybe, he might have a chance. Besides, John told him the interview itself would be a good experience and it might help him prepare for another opportunity down the road.

"It's the first interview on Tuesday morning. Internal applicants got to pick their times, and I wanted to make sure I got the first interview or the last one," Nick said.

"Oh, you have a strategy?" asked his mentor.

"You bet I do," he answered. "You see, I figure the first interview is a prime slot because the committee doesn't have anyone to compare them to yet. The last one is good, as well, because that interview will stay fresh in their mind when they make a decision. Those in the middle probably just get lost in the shuffle."

"Interesting reasoning. I hope it works for you."

"Me, too. I really want this promotion. It'll show that the extra effort I'm putting into my work is paying off. Besides, I don't see another opportunity like this popping up for quite a long time. This might be the only chance I get, so I have to make sure I do everything right," he said.

"Sounds like you really want this," John observed.

"Not only do I want it, I *have* to get it. If I don't, my career might stay in limbo for a long time. I don't want that to happen, so I absolutely *have* to get the promotion. And when I do, I'm celebrating by buying that new car."

"Well, I'm certainly glad to see that you've thought this through and have a plan. However, I detect that you are emotionally attached to the outcome, and from experience I can say that is never a good thing," John offered.

"What do you mean, emotionally attached to the outcome?"

"Nick, perhaps one of my greatest strengths is knowing how to be absolutely committed to an outcome, but not being attached to it. By not being attached, you keep your power, or said the other way, if you are attached, you lose your power. When you are attached, you feel it emotionally, more times than not in your stomach. We can be totally committed to our customer being taken care of and to the desired outcome, but if we are attached to that outcome, it can affect our judgement and actions. Think of doctors; they are committed to helping every patient, right? Now, if they were attached to the outcome, it wouldn't be long before they became a wreck or burned out emotionally. Unfortunately, there will be times when the outcomes for their patients are not what they wish they would be. When emotions come into play, it clouds their thinking. That will happen in every profession, Nick"

"Let me explain it this way—we only have two holes left to play, and right now it's safe to say that I'm probably going to have a lower score than you and will win the round. Now, if I was emotionally attached to that outcome and felt that I absolutely had to win this round, it might affect my game. Rather than playing it safe and playing consistently, I might pull out the big guns and swing harder, hoping to shave a stroke or two on this hole, which I can usually par by playing it safe. But I'd feel it's necessary because I really need to lock in this win right now!"

"But there's a creek that goes across the fairway. If you pulled out a driver here, you'd risk going in the water," Nick pointed out.

"But it would be a risk I'd be willing to take, because if it worked, it would assure me of the outcome that I have to have!" John continued, playing the imaginary scenario out.

"That decision could hurt you, though. If you ended up in the water, you'd actually gain a stroke, and that would set you back even more," Nick said.

"Now you're getting it, son! And if I did go in the water and gained a stroke, what would happen? Well, I still absolutely have to win and won't entertain another possibility, so that means I have to find a way to birdie the next hole, so maybe I would go all in, and …"

"I get where you're going. You'd make rash decisions and take risks you wouldn't normally take, and you probably wouldn't get the results you wanted. Am I right?" Nick smiled.

"Yes, you are. And I want to point out that it can happen to anyone. Even greats like Tiger Woods or Phil Mickelson lose control of their game when they let their emotions affect their decisions and performance. That's also true for work and business. The concept of commitment versus attachment is very important in impacting an outcome. It is the most effective, professional, and powerful way to interact. Let me also add that it gives you leverage, especially when you are dealing with someone who is attached."

"But, John, I really do want this promotion, so what do I do?"

"Commit to it. Just like you committed to saving money to buy a car and just like you committed to learning from me. Work for it, and make it happen. It might not be this time, but it will happen if you are committed to it because you'll do what it takes to make sure it does. The good thing is that you'll do it rationally and thoughtfully, not hastily or in desperation for the outcome that you just have to have. It's commitment that keeps you in control of your thoughts, Nick. On the other hand, it's attachment that lets your thoughts control your outcome."

Ten days later, Nick learned that he had been awarded the promotion, and, again, he had John to thank. He'd walked into the interview with confidence and was armed with a list of his recent and notable accomplishments. Because John had told him that qualifications and experience were only two factors that would be considered, he shared with the interview committee some of the business principles and philosophies he'd learned and was now applying in the workplace. When he was offered the promotion, it was mentioned that those principles were ultimately why he was chosen over the other top candidate.

"We were looking for someone who is capable of leading others, and we like your mindset, Nick," they'd said.

When he called John to let him know the good news, he was enthusiastically congratulated by his mentor.

"So, it looks like your celebration is in order! Are you going out to buy that new car tomorrow?" John asked.

"I've been thinking about that, and I decided not to … just yet."

"Why not? I thought that was the first thing you were going to do?"

"It was. But then I realized that I was emotionally attached to that car and being in a place where I was able to buy it. When I stepped back a bit, I realized that, while it's a fun, sporty ride, I might want to consider something a bit more practical, maybe more suitable for business. Now, I'm glad I took the emotion out of it. While I am committed to buying a new car, maybe it's not *that* car. If you hadn't told me the difference between commitment and attachment, I might have gone in there and bought it on the spot—but I might not have gotten the best deal, the best financing terms, or even the vehicle I wanted. I would have probably accepted whatever was on the lot, even if it didn't have the features I wanted. So I'm going to wait, do a little research, and test drive some other models to see what I really want," said Nick.

"Now you're thinking, Nick ... you've got your head in the game, and you're keeping your emotions out of it. That's precisely what I wanted to see from you. Commit to your dominant thoughts, not your emotions, and you'll get the very best outcome for you," John smiled.

7

THE MINDSET OF SUCCESS

While Nick did possess an increased amount of confidence that stemmed from everything he'd learned from John, he found that in his role as a new sales leader, he had much more learning to do. Not only were his role and his job different than they had been before accepting the promotion, but he found that his perspective also changed over the course of the first six months he'd spent in the position. And John told him that was to be expected, even necessary, given the fact that he was not only responsible for his success, but for the success of his team, as well.

"Bear in mind that there are different meanings of success," his mentor advised. "Among them are increased productivity, profits, and sales. While those are all necessary in a business's overall success, I encourage you to focus more on what it takes to be successful than the actual markers of success."

"Okay, I'm listening. Do tell, what does it really take to be successful?" Nick asked.

"Ninety percent of what it takes to be successful is mindset. You can be or do anything you set your mind to. If you want to be an Olympic athlete, you could be. Sure, it would require a lot of training, commitment, and dedication, but if you wanted it bad enough and had the right mindset, you could make it happen. You could be the VP or CEO of a Fortune 500 company, if that's what you want. But you couldn't do any of that without the right mindset."

"You're saying that mindset is more important than making sound business decisions or even having new, innovative ideas?"

"Those things do help, but they are part of the other ten percent. Like I said, mindset is 90 percent of success. Here's why. Having a strong mindset helps keep you on track when all the 'humanness' creeps in, things like fear, insecurities, concerns, and worries. I learned long ago that those things cloud your judgment and create doubt and uncertainty."

"Wait!" Nick interrupted. "Are you telling me that you ever felt fear or insecurity? If you did, you hid it well, because everyone has always looked up to and respected you. It's been a while since your retirement, and people are still talking about what a great leader you were and the impact you had on the company's success," Nick shared.

"When I was young, much like you, there were times when I second guessed myself and times when I wondered if I was doing the right thing. I became successful because I figured out how to overcome that. I realized something that many great and historic business leaders knew, which is that success requires a positive and strong mindset. A weak or negative mindset will never produce positive results," John stated. "So, I became quite conscious of my mindset and worked to intentionally develop it."

"How did you do that?" Nick inquired.

"First, I was very purposeful about what I watched, listened to, and read. If you put good things into your mind, good things will come out of it. The same is true for the reverse—junk in, junk out, if you know what I mean," the older man smiled. "The thoughts that are dominant, at the forefront and unwavering, are the ones that will steer you and have the greatest impact on your success. The same is true for people. I was also particular about the people I spent time with and chose to be around people who would have a positive impact on me, people who would help me learn and grow. I had the belief that there was much more negative than positive in the world around me, so I had to make sure I was protective of what and who I exposed myself to. Believe me, it made a difference on me and on my success."

"Hey, John, our department is having an informal retreat--you know, a couple days away from the workplace to collaborate as a team. I am in charge of planning it. Do you think it would be a good idea if I incorporated a session about mindset?"

"Absolutely," the mentor readily agreed. "As a matter of fact, I highly recommend it."

"Great, but I'll need your help if I want to give an effective presentation. I want my team to know why it's important, but I think it would be helpful if I share examples of a strong, positive mindset and ways to develop it. Can you help me with that?" asked Nick.

"How about I take you through my journey? These were my thoughts on my mindset. I found that it was necessary to ask myself questions to honestly assess my mindset, things like: do I sanction incompetence in myself, my staff, or anyone around me? Am I as skilled as I need to be to have an unfair advantage? Am I in business with people that I shouldn't be, and, if I am, what is the cost?"

"Oh, that's a good one," the younger man remarked as he jotted down the questions for future reference. "Keep going. Tell me more."

"Okay, am I consistently and constantly going after the top talent? If not, why not? What am I doing on a daily basis to strengthen my mindset?"

"Like reading and learning?" Nick asked.

"Yes, but those are just a couple things one can do. Completing tasks, projects, and goals, exercising, and spending time with positive people are all good examples, as well," John added.

"Those are great questions, and I can already see that I can benefit from asking myself all of them. I'll definitely share them with my team," Nick remarked.

"Very good. Now, don't forget that a strong mindset can benefit from questions, but it will equally benefit from exercising certain principles, essentially making them non-negotiable in your mind," the man said.

"Such as?"

"Oh, Nick, there are many. But I'll share some of my favorites, some that I know have had a profound impact on me," John stated before reciting them one by one:

"Eliminate the option called failure."

"Remember, my ego will not only ruin my business, but it will keep me from doing what I need to."

"And here's a great one to remember at all costs: Negative thinking is always more powerful than positive thinking. Eliminate it."

After pausing briefly to make sure Nick was keeping up with him, John continued.

"I must be unwavering in my desire, in spite of the daily ups and downs. You see, Nick, if your desire wanes, you'll make it easy to give up. You truly have to be committed toward what you want to achieve.

"And here's one that I've found to be extremely helpful: I must work daily to remove the drama around me, personally and professionally. Believe me, drama is a cancer that grows. It can overtake anything good that you've accomplished. My advice is to steer far away from the first sign of drama.

"Um, here's another one. Thinking big is a learned process. I had to learn that. It's not a gift that anyone is born with. You have to learn how to do it, and while that does take time, it becomes easier and more natural once you learn how," John added.

"Interesting. That sounds a lot like being disciplined. I can see where that will help me, as well, especially as my career grows," said Nick.

"It sure will. Now let's move on to some that are more generic, but quite profound when it comes to creating a success-centered mindset. I think they are important for you to implement as a leader and to instill into your team," John said.

"I'm listening," said Nick.

"The first one is an affirmation that I consciously embrace every day. It is: Both my personal and business environments are critical to control in order to have a positive mindset," John stated.

"And the next one is a truth, and the sooner you recognize that it is, the sooner you'll see how effective it is. It is five very powerful words: What we focus on expands. Focus on the good, and more good will come. Focus on the negative and, believe me, you'll see that there is much more where that came from."

"Oh, I like that, and I can already see how I can integrate examples of it into my presentation. Keep going!" Nick exclaimed.

"Okay, here's the next one: Discipline is critical for having and maintaining a strong mindset. Keep in mind, discipline is not negative in this sense. In fact, it lends very positively toward building the right mindset and success. It's all about self-discipline, which, as you pointed out, we've discussed before. It's keeping yourself focused, on track, and committed toward what you want," the mentor shared. "And here's another principle along those same lines: I can build personal power by getting my thinking on track, my values in order, and my body in shape."

"Here is one of my favorites, Nick. A major portion of my success is based upon three words … attitude, approach, and expectations. Let me explain. Attitude is simple; you have to always generate a good, positive attitude. Your approach includes things like preparation, practice, and strategy. And possibly more important, are your expectations. You see, Nick, this presentation will be a product of your attitude; are you going into it with positive thoughts? Are you cognizant of your approach and applying great preparation and practice? And are you going into this with the expectation that you will do great and make a strong, positive impact on the team?" John asked. "Now, let me add one that aligns with that one very well. 'I am in the rejection business; the more I get rejected, the more business I will have.' Do you see how your attitude, approach, and expectations around rejection change from that perspective?"

"I sure do!" Nick answered.

"The last one I want to share with you, Nick, is applicable to everyone, regardless of what they do, where they work, or what's going on in their life. It's the key to universal success, and I don't think anyone can enjoy lasting success without it. It's short and sweet, only four words, but they are four words that I live by."

"What are they?" Nick asked, looking up from the paper he was transcribing his mentor's principles on.

"Strong body, strong mind. The mind and body work together. If one is weak, the other will suffer. If the mind is lazy, the body will be, too. If the body is energetic and healthy, so, too, will be the mind. They work together and depend on each other. You cannot neglect one and expect the other to thrive. That's why I believe in eating right, exercising, and, yes, relaxation and having fun. They're all good for my body and my mind. I only put healthy things that are good for me into my body and my mind. If you do that, you'll set the wheels in motion for success. It worked for me," John attested.

"Wow, this is great! Not only am I learning things that I believe will have a major impact on me and my career, but you've given me something that I can pass on to my team that will benefit them, as well. I have to be honest with you. At first, I dreaded having to make a presentation to my team. All kinds of thoughts went through my head. What if I bomb and it's boring? Heck, I didn't even know what topic to talk about! But now, I'm actually looking forward to going home and working on this presentation while it's still fresh in my mind," Nick said excitedly.

"You'll do fine. Have a positive mindset and give a positive presentation, and you have 90 percent of the ingredients for success," advised the mentor. "Remember, you can't go wrong unless you think you can."

8

DO THE RIGHT THING—ALWAYS

Nick's presentation at the retreat was a resounding success--so much so that the company asked him to prepare a video presentation that could be shared company wide. The simple fact that he received management's approval made him swell with pride. Yet, on the other hand, he was apprehensive. It was a major endeavor, and if he fell short of the standards that were expected, he feared that the approval he'd earned could flip into disapproval quickly. Wanting to prove he was up to the task, he focused the majority of his time on developing the content and presentation of the mindset principles John had taught him.

While he was focusing on his new assignment, he trusted his team to carry out their responsibilities without a great deal of oversight. That was easy; micromanagement had never been his style. His sales staff knew what to do and how to do it. They'd been provided with the right training and resources, and Nick let them know that they had his full support. His door was always open … unless, of course, he was in the middle of taping his presentation.

On a weekly basis, he reviewed his department's reports to make sure they were meeting their expectations and quotas. He routinely communicated incentives and special discounts that would be passed along to their customers. And he always told them he was confident that they'd get the job done. His team didn't disappoint; they strived to continue to meet their expectations and maintain the approval of their supervisor, who they had grown to like and respect. To Nick, nothing could go wrong.

Until it did.

It was at the end of the work week when he sat down to look at his team's reports. His high-performing sales members were consistent—their numbers and results reflected their drive and commitment. They were true professionals who had mastered their profession, and over the years, had become the examples that others looked up to. When there were team members who struggled, they were partnered with these sales pros to receive one-on-one assistance and advice. Learning from the best, like Nick was doing with John, almost always reflected positive results. That was why partnering Seth, a young team member, with Debbie, one of his best salespeople, was how he responded when Seth's sales fell short two weeks in a row.

Seth was a friendly young man who got along well with everyone he met. He also had all of the qualities of a good salesperson. Nick figured he just needed a little personal guidance to get on the right track. He fully entrusted Debbie with the task.

Perusing the reports, he saw that Debbie's sales were consistent with the number of calls she'd logged. That was normal for her; she was as consistent as the day was long. And she held one of the highest rates of conversions in the department.

Turning to Seth, he immediately noticed that the young man had made more than the minimum number of calls, but to Nick's confusion, Seth's sales numbers were still disappointing after two weeks under Debbie's wing. Confused, he logged into the system to take a deeper look at Seth's logs. To the naked eye, everything looked like it was in order, which confused Nick even more. Trying to see if anything stood out, he turned to Debbie's logs. Ten minutes later, he knew exactly what was happening.

Seth was fudging his call numbers. Naturally, if he wasn't making the required number of calls, he wouldn't be able to meet his sales goals. But it wasn't the failure to produce his expected sales that concerned Nick the most. No, it was the fact that Seth was falsifying his reports … and he had the proof right in front of him.

It took Nick a few minutes to figure it out, but when he did, it was blatantly obvious. Seth's call log reflected many of the same numbers that were on Debbie's call log. He wasn't making the contacts, Debbie was. Yet, he documented the duplicate number as a call he had made, as well. This was true for about 25 percent of the calls he logged, which explained why his sales were lower than expected.

Disappointed and uncertain how to approach the situation, Nick was glad he had the weekend before him to figure out what to do.

Torn, he turned to John.

"I'm disappointed, yes, but I keep thinking that he has potential. Maybe there's something going on that I don't know, something that's distracting him and having an impact on his productivity and performance. Maybe he needs additional resources or doesn't fully understand what is expected. If that's the case, I think he deserves another chance," he told his mentor.

"Nick, being a leader means that you sometimes have to make difficult, even unpopular, decisions. Now, if Seth is going through a struggle, he should have told you that the first time you addressed his sales performance. He most certainly should have brought it up when you partnered him with Debbie, don't you think?" John asked.

"Well, yes, I suppose so, but ..."

"No buts, Nick. Whatever the reason, Seth didn't do the right thing, but what he did do has had a negative impact on your other team members and your department as a whole. While everyone else is striving to deliver, he obviously isn't putting in the same effort. And his lack of effort has not only caused his sales to decline, but it's also reduced your entire department's numbers. That reflects on everyone, including you, and it's not fair to those like Debbie who are going above and beyond," John pointed out.

"I get that, but I just wish I knew what to do," Nick sighed.

"I think you know what the right thing to do is. Doing the right thing always works," advised John.

"The right thing for Seth might be to give him another chance," Nick countered.

"Listen, if there is one piece of advice that I want you to heed it's that you should do the right things *always*, not just most of the time. Let's walk through this. Now, when Seth filled out his call log and falsified his numbers, did he do the right thing?" John asked.

"No, he didn't, and I'd like to find out why," Nick replied.

"I'll respond to that with a question, Nick: could there even be a good reason for someone to do that? If you overlook it and give the young man a second or third chance, do you think you'd be doing the right thing—for you, for your team, or even for Seth? Does letting him slide set a good example? Does it support your goals or the efforts of your team?"

"I guess not. I just like him and really think he has promise if I can get to the bottom of what's going on," Nick replied.

"Let's look at this from another perspective. His actions reflect your department as a whole. They are a reflection on you because you are his supervisor. It would be a no-brainer if Seth was trying, but struggling, to meet his quotas. But that's not the case, Nick. He falsified his numbers in order to cover up his lack of effort. Not only does that reflect on *his* integrity, or lack of it, but how you respond to it will also reflect on *your* integrity," the older man informed.

"Nick, I want you to take your emotions completely out of it and listen closely to what I'm about to say because I want it to be the guiding post in everything you do. Son, no risk or amount of money is worth your integrity. This is true 100 percent of the time, whether someone is watching or not. Seth probably never thought anyone would look closely at his reports, so he felt safe in falsifying them. He'll regret that, and he will learn from it, I assure you. But when you do the right thing, there aren't any regrets. When you always tell the truth, do what you say you are going to do, and make decisions based on the right thing to do, you never have to look back, put energy into worrying, or risk negative consequences. In this instance, you haven't done anything wrong, but your response to it can send a message that you'll regret. By submitting false logs, he betrayed your trust and the trust of his fellow team members. Would it be right or fair for the rest of your staff to overlook that?"

"I guess not," Nick answered with resignation.

"It's all about integrity, Nick. You have to understand that we are our word. Honoring your word by being your word is always, always the path you must choose to follow. When you do, you'll be known for your integrity, which is the quality of being honest and having strong moral principles, moral uprightness. Believe me, that will earn you the respect of your team, and people will be able to trust that you'll always do the right thing for them," said John.

"The answer is really quite simple. Just as Seth had a choice before he chose to submit a false report, you have a choice in how you respond to it. Did Seth do the right thing? I think we can both agree that he did not. The way you respond to it can set the standard for your entire department. If you let it slide, your team might not feel like you have their back. But if you do the right thing for yourself, your team, and the company, you'll set the expectations that you demand in the future—from yourself and from those under your supervision. When that happens, you can enjoy the state of being whole and undivided," John shared.

"Thanks, John, you've been really helpful. As much as I don't look forward to it, I know what I have to do," admitted Nick.

"The good thing, Nick, is that when you do the right thing, you never have to wonder if it was the right thing or not. You won't second guess yourself or regret your decisions or actions later. Look at it this way, doing the wrong thing is difficult. It weaves a web of dishonesty and distrust. But when you do the right thing, it's easy. There are no excuses to be made or anything to cover up that could haunt you later. It's always right, no matter what. That's because the right thing is *always* the right thing; it never changes. Do the right thing, always, unapologetically and without regret, and people will always know what to expect from you and what you expect from them. You'll find that by 'making doing the right thing' one of your unflinching values, it becomes a dominant thought that impacts every decision you make. You'll never again have to ask, 'What should I do?' because you will *know* you're doing the right thing. That's when you know you're a man of your word and a man of integrity," said John.

"Well, I have had a great role model," Nick smiled. "I trust that you wouldn't steer me wrong."

"Now, that wouldn't be the right thing to do, would it?" John teased.

9

PAY ATTENTION

Nick was getting settled in his role as a supervisor, and he found that he enjoyed it. He had a good camaraderie with his team and took extra care to make sure they knew he was there for them. He knew that their success depended on his support and guidance, so maintaining positive relationships with his team was one of his highest priorities.

His team responded well to his management style, and it was reflected in their sales numbers. His department consistently met their expectations, even exceeding them in several quarters. It was a trend he was proud of and one that he hoped would continue for the foreseeable future.

But it didn't. For some reason, their numbers fell—not drastically, but enough to cause concern. As he contemplated the reasons why, he couldn't isolate an obvious answer.

"I just can't put my finger on it," he told John.

"From experience, I can tell you that there is a reason. There has to be. You just haven't uncovered it yet," his mentor said.

"I know. What I don't know, though, is how to find the reason. Sure, there are small things that can all contribute toward a decline or plateau in our numbers, but I can't help but think that there must be something more going on. As the former owner of the company, what would you suggest I do?" asked Nick.

"Pay attention," John said.

"I am," Nick replied.

"Well, while it's good to know that you are paying attention to my advice, that's not what I meant when I told you to pay attention. Nick, I mean that my advice to you is to pay attention—really pay attention to what your staff is saying. Even more important, though, is the need to pay very close attention to what they are *not* saying."

"How can I pay attention to something that is not being said?" asked the confused young man.

"Let's just say that you can learn as much, if not more, by standing back and observing than by talking and asking questions," John said. "This is as true for you as it is for your team."

"I'm not sure I'm following you, John," Nick admitted.

"That's understandable. Maybe an example will help. It all stems around the fact that observation is an excellent instructor. This is something I learned when I was just a young boy. My family had taken a trip to Hawaii when I discovered that I actually learn best by watching and observing. We were on Waikiki Beach, which, by the way, is beautiful if you've never had the good fortune to experience it. Anyway, my parents rented me a surfboard, but I didn't really have any experience, and I knew it. Now, most young boys probably wouldn't waste a second before throwing their surfboard into the ocean and giving it a shot, I decided to do the opposite. I sat on my surfboard on dry land and did nothing but watch the older boys and men surf. It was apparent that they really knew what they were doing, and I thought maybe I could learn something by watching them."

"Did you?" asked Nick.

"Oh, boy, did I!" John grinned. "After watching and paying attention to everything they did, from the moment they rode their board out to the moment that they timed the waves and stood on the board, using their arms to balance themselves, they taught me so much. I know that they say the best education is experience and hands-on learning, but observation is just as important. After spending some time really paying attention to skilled surfers, I decided I was ready to give it a try. I paddled out and watched some more, up close, and to my parents' amazement, as well as my own, I actually began to ride the waves in. And it was just as thrilling as I thought it would be, but if I hadn't watched others first, I might have jumped in blind and quickly become frustrated. In that case, it wouldn't have been such a great experience, would it?"

"I guess not," Nick agreed. "So you're telling me to watch and listen to my team, and maybe I'll learn what they're doing right?"

"Not exactly. Let's just say that being present and observant allows you to learn a lot. People will show you who they are if you pay attention, Nick. Your team will show you what their problems are if you step back and observe them. I'm not talking about asking questions and hoping you'll get answers. More often than not, you won't get them. This is about being present and paying attention, because when that happens, you'll start to hear what they *aren't* saying. Think about it. Your team isn't likely to tell you that they resent their quotas being raised or that their self-esteem has taken a hit, are they? There are just some times that you won't get a forthright and honest answer," explained John. "But by simply being observant and listening, really listening to what they're saying and not saying, you'll discover so much that you didn't know."

"Such as?"

"Well, just by watching, you can tell a lot about someone's attitude. Are they being defensive? Resentful? Do they appear to be anxious and stressed? Is there a lack of motivation that wasn't there before?"

"Okay, I get that. Now, what do you mean when you say I can hear what they aren't saying?" Nick asked.

"When you ask them if they have any issues or need support, the answers might be in what they aren't telling you. Perhaps there is something they are embarrassed to tell you, or maybe it's something that they don't think is important, but it could play a role. It's your job to sit back and pay attention so you can get the information you need. I might add that this is also something that is true for prospects," John told him.

"Prospects? How so?" asked Nick.

"It's only natural to assume that if sales are struggling, your sales team is a factor, but so, too, are their prospects. Nick, we've all been there. We've given a flawless sales presentation to what we believe is an interested prospect, only to hear at the end that they 'aren't interested, have to think about it,' or the one nobody wants to hear: 'not today.' I mean, what does that mean? Does it mean not today, but tomorrow? Next month? Next year? Or worse, never?"

"Yes, nobody knows how to interpret that one," Nick agreed.

"You see, Nick, my point is that it's not what the prospect is telling you. It's what they're *not* telling you. Do you remember the classic sales scenario where a young couple comes in to buy a new car and the salesman tries to sell the husband the newest, most expensive sports car on the floor, failing to even notice that the wife is obviously pregnant? He's not offering them a solution to their problem; he's simply trying to reach a quota, win a contest, or earn a higher commission. In this case, it's obvious that he's not paying attention, but if he did, he'd learn pretty quickly why the prospect isn't buying," John explained.

"I've heard that one before. It's pretty obvious, but it makes the point," Nick shared.

"Okay, so let's look at another scenario. Let's say that we have a salesman named Sal, and Sal sells swimming pools. He makes an appointment with a suburban housewife, a mother of three kids under the age of five. From the moment he walks into their home, the woman is constantly distracted. One of the kids is clinging to her and refusing to let go, another one spills their milk and she has to rush to clean that up, and then the baby wakes up from its nap and is crying in her crib. Then there are other distractions: the phone rings or she gets a text and needs to check it. She has to wipe a runny nose. You get the idea," John said.

"Oh yes, I've had similar appointments," Nick laughed.

"Okay, so during this whole time, Sal is getting his sales pitch in. He talks about how much fun a swimming pool is. The kids will absolutely love it! They'll never want to come inside the house again. They'll be the most popular kids in the neighborhood, and they'll never lack for friends to play with. He tells her to imagine her backyard with a pool full of kids from down the block and around the corner. Getting a pool would earn her the Mom of the Year Award!" John said.

"But that's not going to get Sal a sale, Nick," John added. "And for a really good reason. Sal isn't paying attention. He's not listening to what this mother is not telling him."

"What's that?" Nick asked, curious.

"If he was really paying attention, he'd know that the last thing this mother wants is more kids running around, adding to the already non-stop demands she's dealing with every single day," John advised.

"So you're saying she's not a good prospect for a pool, right?" Nick surmised.

"Not at all. In this instance, Sal just isn't giving her the solution to *her* problems. You see, what she really needs and would be willing to pay for is relaxation. She'd be willing to pay for calm, quiet time. By being observant, he'd see what she's not telling him, and he'd take another approach, selling a pool as a relaxing getaway in her own backyard, where she can float her cares away.

Can you see in this instance that being observant actually gives you the answers you want? In sales, those are the answers you really need. You won't get those answers in canned excuses for not buying. It's what the customer isn't telling you that matters, and if you pay attention, you'll discover what that is, sometimes rather quickly," the older man advised.

"So it's all about non-verbal communication," Nick summarized.

"Oh, not all of it. Communication is and always will be vital. Without open, honest communication, every relationship will struggle and decline. That is true with friends, family members, business partners, colleagues, and prospects. Sometimes paying attention helps with verbal communication, especially if someone says something unexpected or out of their norm, leaving you wondering why they might have said what they did or said it in a certain way. If you really listen and stop talking, you'll often find out what their reason or motive might be," John explained.

"In the end, Nick, it's about *effective* communication, whether it is verbal or non-verbal. Paying attention and being observant to what is being said and what isn't being said will enhance your communication and ability to respond and connect with people. When you give yourself the opportunity to discover that you can learn more by watching and listening than you can by simply asking questions alone, you'll find the answers to your sales issues and will then be in a position to find the right solution," John suggested.

"John, I think it might be helpful if I bring this up at our next staff meeting, especially as it relates to prospective buyers. Pay attention, watch, and listen to what the prospect isn't telling you. That's when you'll find the solution to their problem," Nick said.

"That's an excellent idea. And I have another idea that might help you address your sales slump. If you're available, Nick, I'd like you to join me and a couple of my former colleagues for breakfast this Saturday. Nothing fancy, just good food and good company. I think they might be able to shed some light on your situation from a different angle."

"I'd like that, John. I'm willing to listen to any suggestions or ideas," Nick responded.

"Great. Meet us at Rosie's Diner on the corner of Oak and Jefferson Street next Saturday morning at 8:00 sharp. Don't be late."

"No way! You taught me that the very first time I reached out to you. Believe me, I paid attention," Nick laughed.

10

UNDER PROMISE AND OVER DELIVER

When Nick walked into Rosie's Diner at 7:55 a.m., he wasn't surprised to find that John and his two colleagues were already seated at a table.

How does he do it every single time? he wondered. *It's like a game to him, making sure that he's always the first to arrive. Even when I try to beat him at his game, he's one up on me.*

Sighing, Nick resigned himself to the fact that John was a pro, one who had mastered this game long before they'd met, and it was probably better that he accept the fact that he wasn't ever going to win the unspoken challenge. Still, the competitive side of him hoped that one day he would.

"Nick, you're right on time. Here, have a seat," John said, motioning to the empty chair next to him.

Nick pulled back the sturdy wooden chair, noticing that its color was worn and faded in several places on the seat and back. As he looked around the small restaurant, he noticed that it was a typical nondescript diner, much like any you'd see on any Main Street across the country. It was simple and clean, with a homey atmosphere. But despite its lack of design and upscale decor, the place was packed.

"Good thing we got here when we did, or we might not have gotten a table," he remarked. "Is it always this busy?"

"Oh, yes, this little cafe draws a crowd, mostly repeat customers who come back because they know they'll have a great meal every time. Many of the folks here are regulars," said John. "Now, Nick, I'd like to introduce you to my friends, Chloe and Gavin. I've known them for years. In fact, they both used to work for me and our company."

"It's good to meet you," Nick replied. "As John mentioned, you both worked for him at one time. What did you do, and what do you do now, if I can ask?"

"Sure," Gavin replied. "I was a senior sales representative until I left to accept a position as regional sales director in healthcare, specifically medical equipment."

"And I was VP of Sales and Marketing before I left the company to venture into commercial real estate. Today, I am the owner and CEO of a real estate development company," Chloe shared.

Just then, their server arrived, greeting them with a bright smile and sunny demeanor. After filling their water glasses and coffee cups, she sat a plate of pastries and a bowl of fresh mixed fruit in the center of the table.

"Help yourself," John motioned toward the food.

"You already ordered?" asked Nick.

"Oh, no. It's complimentary, one of the reasons this place is always busy. Did you notice that you didn't have to request water, like you do in most places nowadays? You'll also find that you'll never have to ask for a refill in your coffee cup. The service is nothing short of excellent," John said.

"I don't know how they can afford to do this. Aren't they taking a risk that people will eat the free pastries and fruit and not order anything on the menu?" Nick asked.

"Some might think so, but from a different perspective, isn't it possible that it's this level of service that keeps this establishment at full capacity?" John posed.

"Hmm, I never thought of it that way," Nick admitted. "It's obvious that something is working for them."

Nick listened as John and his colleagues brought each other up to date on their lives and experiences since the last time they'd met. Intermittently, they'd stop to explain something to Nick so he could understand what they were referring to in their conversation. From what Nick gathered, Chloe and Gavin had both worked with John, and under his supervision, they had grown and risen in his company. They'd remained friends long after they'd left the company for other opportunities, and the three now formed an informal small mastermind group. These breakfasts were their monthly meetings where they'd brainstorm ideas and keep each other up to date on their challenges and successes.

To Nick, the conversation was fascinating. He was content to listen and found that he learned a lot by their back-and-forth exchange. What they were saying was insightful, but he found that what they weren't saying also shone through. By paying attention, he could tell that the trio not only were great friends, but they also had immense professional respect for each other and valued each other's opinions and input. Most of all, Nick was in awe at the combined years of experience that they brought with them. That equaled a lot of wisdom, and he wanted to gain as much of it as he could while he was in their company.

Their server arrived, with plates stacked on both arms, each containing a portion of food that could only be described as very generous. Without any hesitation, she placed the right order in front of the right person, making sure they had whipped butter, jam, and hot biscuits fresh from the oven, before refilling their water glasses and coffee mugs. Considering the number and variety of plates on the table, Nick was amazed that she kept their orders straight and didn't overlook a single detail.

Stopping only to briefly thank and converse with their server, the trio continued their conversation while they ate. When they finished with "old business," John turned to Nick.

"I hope you don't mind, Nick, but I took the liberty of bringing Gavin and Chloe up to speed with your current sales situation. I thought they might have some additional insight that could help you and your team. Why don't you explain your situation in your own terms?" John invited.

Nick carefully informed them about their recent slump and then went on to share what he thought was behind it, admitting that he didn't have all the answers. He told them what he'd addressed and what he didn't feel the problem was, as well.

"The team is all meeting their call numbers. However, the conversion rate isn't what it should be. I've observed their presentation, and they are diligent about making sure prospects have all the information before them. They let them know how great our company is and that we stand by what we sell more than anyone else. They really do talk us up to prospects, so I don't think that's the issue. Frankly, I'm not sure what the barrier is. If you have any thoughts, I'd welcome them. I'm open to anything right now," Nick said.

Across the table, Chloe and Gavin exchanged looks. It was Chloe who spoke first.

"If it's okay, Gavin, I'll go first. Nick, I know that you're looking at this barrier from different angles. One, it could be that your team is lacking something it needs at this time. That could be motivation or inspiration or even an incentive. Two, it could be something your team is or isn't doing that is creating a barrier to closing a sale. I'd like to focus on what your team *is* doing, if I may," she said.

"Of course," Nick nodded.

"You say that your sales team talks the company up. I imagine they're letting prospects know that your company is better than the competition and telling them every advantage and benefit they'll get when they become a customer. Am I right?"

"Yes, for the most part. The sales team is well trained in the benefits we offer our clients and our value proposition," Nick agreed.

"Have you considered that that might just be part of the problem?" she asked.

"What? I'm not certain I understand what you're getting at," he admitted.

"Well, maybe they are over promising, but under delivering, when, in fact, it should be the opposite: under promising and over delivering." she said, pausing for effect.

"Why would we under promise? That's contrary to everything I learned in sales training," Nick asked in confusion.

"She's right, Nick," John interjected. "These are two key components to winning with customers and colleagues that I learned by trial and error. Once you hear her out, I think you'll agree."

"Thank you, John," Chloe smiled. "Now, where do I begin? Nick, I learned early on not only the value of happy clients, but how much better it was dealing with happy people than it was with upset people. Many salespeople or service providers make the critical error of over promising. Usually, this is not done to help their company, but to benefit them personally or for some other self-serving reason. In a sales situation, most people can sense this, and it turns them off. Then when they fail to deliver as promised, the customer is left disappointed. I've found, though, that the opposite is true: the easiest way to create happy clients is to set their expectations, then to make sure I exceeded them."

"Interesting," Nick said. "I'd like to hear how that works if you can elaborate."

"Sure. You see, everyone has expectations, expressed or not. If you don't set expectations, you have little chance of meeting or exceeding them. Just like you can't meet a goal you don't set. You cannot meet an expectation if you don't know what the expectations are. Makes sense, doesn't it?" Chloe asked. "On the other hand, when we tell people what to expect, or explain what the possible outcomes are, we provide them with clarity or at the very least tell them what they can expect to anticipate. This allows us to know what we can do or need to do in order to surprise or delight the individual, whether it is our customer or partner."

"Why do we want to surprise the customer? I thought telling them upfront what we promise to deliver means there are no surprises," Nick interjected.

"I've got this, Chloe," Gavin volunteered. "By surprise, Chloe is referring to a positive surprise, meaning that the customer didn't expect us to impress them so much. That's where under-promising comes in. In my opinion, the belief that we need to over promise and build ourselves up to the sky is misguided. However, it's been pounded into many a salesperson's minds, even if it doesn't work. I tell my teams to flip it and make under promising the dominant thought that steers their interactions. Nick, I think you'll agree that when we over promise, we risk letting the customer down and leaving them disappointed because, in their opinion, we didn't deliver the level or quality that we promised and what they expected. Now let's flip that around and go with under promising, and over delivering, which is something I do in every sale. I tell them the unconditionals—this is what you'll get with us. These are our non-negotiable deliverables. Those stand for themselves and are part of our sales presentation. But I don't tell them all the extras they'll get, like my personal promise to follow up with them every single week and a responsiveness that is unparalleled in the industry. Imagine their delight when they switch from a company that took their money and disappointed them to one that can't do enough for them after they become a customer. Whether it's a loyalty discount, an unexpected thank-you, or a birthday gift, I go out of my way to surprise my customers and give them more than they expect."

It was John who spoke up next.

"In the simplest terms, Nick, this means that you and your staff should always do more than you say you will, which is the premise of under-promising and over-delivering. It's a concept that's easy to execute, but all too often is overlooked. Impressing, even wowing, your customers will not only earn customer loyalty and their repeat business, but it will have a significant impact on referrals," John advised. "If you want to know that it works, you only have to look around you. Rosie's epitomizes this concept, and judging by the fact that every chair is full, I'd say it's working quite well for them."

"Well, I have to agree that they over deliver," Nick said, nodding toward his half-full plate of food. "I think they gave me two meals! And that's on top of the fruit and pastries we enjoyed before breakfast! But I have to admit that I don't know how they under promise."

"Take a look around, Nick," Gavin said. "It's a mom-and-pop diner, nothing special at first glance. They don't have fancy tables and fine linens. Just great food and lots of it. There's nothing on the front of the building that boasts that they have the best breakfast in town, just a sign that says, 'Good food at good prices.' Now, that's under promising if I ever heard it."

"That's right," Chloe continued. "And their menu doesn't tell you that their sausage is homemade and perfectly seasoned or that their eggs are fresh from the farm every day. Or that they grind and brew their own coffee, or that they have the fluffiest pancakes this side of the Mississippi. So while someone walks in and expects to have a homestyle breakfast, they don't have any idea that they're about to have one of the best breakfasts they've ever had."

"And a *lot* of it," John added. "And let's not forget that it's served by the friendliest staff who really make you feel like they like you and want you to have a great experience. They don't promise you any of that, but they sure do deliver it! That's under promising and over delivering, Nick, and it's the reason we come back here every month."

"Well, I know I'll be back," Nick said.

"The point is, Nick, that perhaps your competition is already under promising and over delivering and word is getting out that they are. In that case, you do have some work to do to turn that around. Even if that isn't the situation, I think it will benefit you and your team to identify ways that you can implement this practice in your department. Set the expectations, then find ways to wow your customers by going above and beyond those expectations," John suggested.

"I'm already getting a few ideas. Actually, I'm excited to talk to my team about it. I think it will inspire and motivate them, and that may be the push they need," Nick said.

"The added bonus, Nick, is that when you have happy clients, you don't have the negative publicity from upset clients … and you don't need to spend valuable time addressing and correcting complaints. That leaves you with more time to find more customers to make happy!" exclaimed Chloe.

"It sounds like a win-win, that's for sure," Nick agreed.

"So do you have any ideas on how you can over deliver to your customers?" asked Gavin.

"Well, I'm going to start by bringing my team to Rosie's for breakfast so they can see this practice at work. Maybe we can also give our customers an unexpected gift as a thank you for their business," Nick said, thinking out loud.

"That sounds like a good start," asked John.

"Who knows? Maybe we'll thank them for their business with a gift card to Rosie's. That way, we over deliver and delight our customers, and they also get to be delighted by having breakfast at the best little diner in town," Nick said.

"I think you might be onto something," John laughed. "And it sounds like you're a happy Rosie's customer, too. You've just witnessed firsthand this practice at work. Now you know how your customers will feel when your team under promises and over delivers. Find a way to make your customers happier than they expect to be, and it will be reflected in sales. When your customers are happy, you can't go wrong."

11

HAVE FUN

Over the course of the next several months, Nick and his team identified ways to over deliver to their customers, and as John, Chloe, and Gavin predicted, it had a positive impact on sales. To Nick's delight, it also had a positive impact on his sales team. As they experienced positive results, he noticed that the discouragement that had been spreading through the department waned and was replaced by optimism and inspiration to find additional ways to make their customers happy.

Nick wasn't able to identify one specific area that had caused their sales to struggle, and eventually he accepted the fact that there were likely multiple factors. By making a few changes, they were able to see an uptick in sales, which was reflected in his team's attitude and confidence. No longer discouraged, they were encouraged to do more and be better. And even more, because Nick encouraged them to be actively involved in finding the answers, he found that the team actually enjoyed being part of the solution.

As the months passed, Nick was increasingly motivated to exceed expectations and set new, higher ones. John observed him and felt proud that he played a role in the development of such an ambitious and driven young man. He'd come a long way from the young employee who ran out to the parking lot to make sure the retiring CEO didn't leave without his cake. He'd grown immensely from the hesitant salesperson who went out on a limb to ask the company's owner and CEO to share his success secrets.

As John mentored Nick, he grew to know a lot about the young executive. He knew what Nick wanted for his department, his company, and his team, but it was time to focus on something just as important: what Nick wanted for himself.

It was a conversation that John felt they needed to have, and he knew just where to have it.

"Nick, can you meet me at the Gold Shea Restaurant Friday at noon?" he asked. "Oh, and can you bring something with you?"

"What are you thinking of? A brown rabbit?" Nick smiled as he spoke into the phone.

"No, we've already done the rabbit, if I recall," John chuckled. "How about this time you bring something fun?"

"Like what?" Nick asked, hoping for clarification.

"That's up to you to decide," John quipped.

"Well, what's fun for me might not be fun for you," Nick pointed out.

"Precisely," was the only reply he got.

* * *

"Something fun, something fun," Nick said to himself as he walked through his house looking for something that would shout out FUN to him, but nothing spoke. There were a couple magazines laying on the coffee table, a candle in the foyer, and a large plant in the corner that he often forgot to water. In his bedroom, there was a clock on the nightstand, the ever-ready remote control, and a phone charger. But nowhere in his home could he find anything that could be described as "fun."

Then he remembered that he had tennis rackets in the trunk of his car, but truth be told, he'd lost interest and stopped playing years before. He could lie and bring one just so he didn't walk in empty handed, but that wouldn't be the right thing to do. Besides, he had a feeling he wouldn't be able to fool John, at least not that easily. The man had an uncanny way of seeing through him.

With no inspiration, he took a trip to a department store, hoping something would spark his imagination. Though he could play video games, he dismissed them. He wasn't really into them, like some of his friends. He enjoyed playing cards, but poker and euchre were games of strategy. They were challenging, yes, but they didn't meet his definition of fun. As he strolled the aisles, he recalled playing darts, bicycling, and other pastimes he'd enjoyed as a teenager, but not lately.

Hmmm, look, there's a joke book, he thought. *Maybe John will think that's fun. But wait, is it supposed to be fun for me … or for him?*

As Nick's mind wandered, trying to think of something, *anything,* that he would qualify as fun, he suddenly remembered how much he used to enjoy snow skiing, another thing he hadn't done for years. After all, the climate wasn't favorable for snow in their area. In fact, it was a rarity. But the few times he had visited a ski resort, he'd had a blast. There was something so exhilarating about flying down a mountain covered with snow; it was like flying with your feet on the ground.

That triggered other thoughts about how much fun he'd had when he went hang gliding with his buddies and the one time he'd gone bungee jumping. Like skiing, these sports left him with a thrill that he didn't get every day, and he couldn't deny that every time he had enjoyed them, he'd had fun, lots of fun.

Walking out of the store empty handed, he finally settled on printing some photographs he downloaded from the Internet that showed people enjoying the very same activities that gave him a thrill.

That Friday, he walked into the Gold Shea precisely ten minutes early and immediately spotted John, who waved his hand from across the room to get his attention.

"Hey, John, it's great to see that you're on time, as always," he teased.

"You, as well. I'm pleased to see that you're making progress. Ten minutes early–I'm impressed," John countered. "So now that you're here, did you remember to bring something? Something fun?"

"Umm, yes," Nick said, pulling the photos out of his breast pocket. "But I'm not so sure you'll think they're fun."

"Let's see–downhill snow skiing and, oh, hang gliding. Not quite what I expected, but ..." John said.

"That's just it, John. I wasn't sure what you were looking for, either," Nick stated.

"I didn't know what I was looking for ... and for good reason. You see, Nick, it occurred to me that, although I've been mentoring you for some time now, I don't know what you enjoy, besides working, that is. I sincerely believe that I'd be doing you an injustice if I focused only on your career in our time together. It wouldn't be fair to you at all," John explained.

"I still don't understand," said Nick.

"Let me preface what I'm about to say with something I firmly believe. There is no dress rehearsal; this is our life. We must find joy and enjoyment, whether it is at work or during our free time in whatever we are doing. Both areas are equally important. A great deal of our time is spent on the job, and if we don't have fun or at least find some real joy in what we're doing, that would be a shame. Think about it! How sad and unfortunate it must be during all of those hours, days, and even years if you aren't happy or having any fun at all," John said.

"I do like what I'm doing," Nick nodded.

"And that's great. But I am aware that sales can be stressful. There are times when there is a lot of pressure to meet quotas. Those things can really take a toll on us. I know it's cliche, but laughter can really be the best medicine. I want to encourage you to find ways to have fun at work and at play. Being able to have fun and enjoy things during my free time is one of the reasons I worked,

Nick. I wanted to be able to have the time and money to have fun, play golf, enjoy taking my family on vacation, and even being able to play with my grandchildren without being glued to my phone for fear of missing a phone call. It's rare that I ever hear you mention doing anything fun, young man, and that's why I wanted to address this issue," John explained.

"I admit that I've been very focused on my career since we met. I don't want to slack and lose my window of opportunity. I guess I always figured that if I concentrate on my career now, there will be time for fun later," admitted Nick.

"That's my point. It doesn't have to be one or the other. I don't want you to sacrifice what brings you joy and enjoyment in life for your career. Work will always be there–I promise you that. But your friends and family members may not. Your ability to do the things that you consider fun might also be affected as the years pass. I learned that years ago, and, thankfully, realized that there was nothing wrong with enjoying my job and also taking time to enjoy my favorite hobbies."

"Fun things? Like hang gliding?" Nick affirmed.

"For you, perhaps, but hang gliding is a little too daring for me," John laughed. "That validates my point that fun is subject to interpretation. To me, it means whatever brings you joy. That could be a walk on the beach with someone you love. It could be gardening, playing sports, or simply watching a football game with some good buddies. It might be going to an escape room or a comedy club. It can be something that makes you laugh hysterically or simply brings a warm feeling to your heart. The point is to find those moments and days and really experience them. Otherwise, what are you working for?" John asked.

"You're talking about work-life balance, right?"

"To be honest, Nick, I'm not sure what that really is. What I'm talking about is making it fun. Sure, you can be successful without being happy, and you can actually be happy without being very successful. But why would you do either if you have the wonderful opportunity to do both? You can have fun at work, and if you don't think so, just pick up the book, FISH, by Harry Paul. If a bunch of guys can make a fish market so much fun that watching becomes a tourist attraction and spectator sport, anyone can find ways to bring fun into the workplace. Nick, imagine how much your team will enjoy coming to work if it's a place where they can earn a living and find joy! Imagine how much you'll enjoy working with them, and then go one step further and imagine how such an environment would affect their performance!" John said with excitement.

"Did you do that, John?" Nick asked.

"Not every day, but I did make an effort to create an atmosphere where people were free to laugh and have fun while they did their job. There were times when I even discouraged anyone from taking their work home with them. Life is too short to spend it all working, Nick. From experience, I can tell you that you can't regain lost time. Once it's gone, it cannot be recaptured. Like I said, you only get one shot to create a life that you love. There are no do-overs. I would be remiss if I stood by idly while you focused on work, work, work, and then one day realized that you never took the chance to experience the things you enjoy, like skiing and hang gliding," John told him.

"Or having a puppy," Nick added.

"What?"

"A puppy. I've always wanted one, but my parents wouldn't let me have one when I was growing up. They said we weren't home enough. But I've been thinking about getting one more and more lately, and when you mentioned that I should experience things that would bring me joy, I was reminded of that," Nick admitted.

"See what I mean? Life has a way of telling you what you need," John noted.

"Maybe so. I'll have to think about it."

"You know, one of the greatest things that ever happened to me was the most spontaneous thing I'd ever done," John shared.

"What was that?" asked the younger man.

"I got down on one knee and asked the greatest woman in the world to be my wife. I didn't see it coming; it just happened. We were having a great time, and I just knew it was right. And I have never once wondered if I did the right thing," John smiled.

"No regrets, huh?" Nick grinned back at his mentor.

"Not a single one. And that's what I want for you, Nick– a career and a life without regrets, one that brings you joy while you're living it and enjoyment when you look back on it," the former CEO said, hoping that the young sales supervisor took his words to heart.

12

DOMINANT THOUGHTS

The two men worked together, meeting almost every week for two years while Nick gained experience. In their third year together as mentor and mentee, John invited Nick to join his mastermind group and found that he contributed valuable input and added a fresh perspective into their meetings, which were still always held at their favorite restaurant, Rosie's.

By this time, Nick had been promoted to District Sales Manager at B.A.M. Enterprises, a role in which he changed the dynamics of their sales teams company wide. With every new sales goal, he created a new initiative, making sure it was always fun and always rewarding. Sure, there were company benefits and rewards for meeting goals, but Nick sweetened the pot by announcing that the winner would get to choose the team's "fun day." It was a hit among their sales teams, and the winners showed their imaginations in choosing the events and experiences. Sometimes, they'd proclaim it to be a day at the beach. Other winners had opted to spend an afternoon bowling or playing billiards. Still another signed them up for dinner and a movie, and one even registered them all for an authentic pizza cooking class that, surprisingly to some, had become one of their all-time favorites.

To Nick's surprise, employee retention increased and so did their sales numbers. It was a win-win, and he had to admit that John was right–having fun at work was enjoyable for everyone, even him. And the bonus was that it was one of the reasons he earned his promotion. His incentives had gained notice with C-level executives, so much so that they wanted him to implement some of them across the board.

However, he never lost sight of results and found himself incorporating many of John's teachings when coaching his teams. He had even created a training program out of them, calling them Dominant Thoughts.

"What you think will always have an impact on your actions, behaviors, and results," he shared. "And the thoughts that will have the greatest impact are those that are the most dominant. If you believe a goal is unachievable, your actions will follow your thoughts. If you think you can't do something, you'll be right because you won't try or will only give it a halfhearted attempt," he told his audience.

From there, he had his team members write down the thoughts that were most dominant at that time. It didn't matter if they were positive or negative, he explained. Positive thoughts were important because they needed to be reinforced, and negative thoughts were just as significant because they needed to be replaced with thoughts that were aligned toward the results they wanted, not the results they didn't want.

It was something he'd learned from his time spent with John. His mentor wasn't teaching him what to do, but instead, he was teaching him how to think because, as he explained it, success didn't happen by chance –it has always been and will always be spurred by a thought, which creates an attitude, which triggers action.

After his fourth quarter in a row of exceeding sales goals, Nick was offered the position of Vice President of Sales for M.A.B., a role he once didn't think would ever be in the realm of possibility. But with John's encouragement and guidance, he'd not only reached that pinnacle, but he'd actually grown to believe that his future held even more beyond that. Confident in his abilities, Nick had become a leader, one others now looked up to in much the same way he had once looked up to John when he was a young sales professional.

And even more surprising to the rising young executive was the fact that he now spent more time doing the things he enjoyed than he had at any time in his life. Whether he was throwing a ball to his golden retriever, Sunny, renovating their future home with his fiance, Brooke, or spending an afternoon at the baseball stadium with his friends, Nick was enjoying the life he had created and didn't have a single regret.

"John, I can't thank you enough. Five years ago, I wanted to know the secret to your success, and naive as I was, I actually thought you would tell me right then and there in the parking lot," Nick laughed. "I never dreamed that by asking one question, I would have had the opportunity to learn so much from you. What I do know is that if someone asked me the secret to *my* success, I would be able to tell them it was you and your mentorship."

"It was never me," John said. "It was always you. No one is responsible for your success but you, Nick. I just gave you some things to think about. Remember when I told you that 90 percent of what it takes to be successful is mindset? It was you who created a success mindset, did the work, and turned those thoughts into results. Like I told you when we first met, you had to be committed to doing what was necessary. Otherwise, my mentorship wouldn't have made any difference at all."

Nick's mind went back to that commitment and the "test" John had put him through to make sure he was willing to do what others weren't. The 10:10 phone call, not once, not twice, but three days in a row, and then the bizarre request for him to bring a gift card and a rabbit with him. The memory made him smile.

"What's so amusing?" asked his friend.

"Oh, I was just thinking about how far I've come since the day we met. I just hope one day to be able to pay it forward and share what you've taught me with someone else," Nick smiled.

"You will," John assured him. "As long as your mind is set on it, it will happen. All you have to do is plant the seed in your mind, and if you tend to it, it will grow. When it becomes dominant, it will cause you to take action and steer you toward that one person who will truly benefit from your mentorship."

"Is that what happened when we met? Did your thoughts steer you toward me, a young, green sales representative who didn't have a clue?" Nick grinned.

"Let's just say, my friend, that there was a reason I 'forgot' to have a piece of my retirement cake. No longer CEO, my thoughts had already shifted toward my future plans, which included helping others achieve the same success I had enjoyed for decades. And it was then that you showed up—actually, your timing couldn't have been better," John said with a slow grin.

Nick laughed and gave John a friendly slap on the back. While he knew John would never let him beat him at "his game," he also knew what John wasn't saying—for the first time, he was letting him know that he thought they were equal. To Nick, that was a great thought, indeed.

DOMINANT

THOUGHTS

CHAPTER BY CHAPTER

DOMINANT THOUGHTS: CHAPTER BY CHAPTER

1
THE BIG QUESTION

- The person who finds the answers they seek is the person who is not afraid to ask questions. Throughout history, questions have been the keys that unlock the secrets to success.
- You must be willing to do what others aren't if you want to have what others don't.
- Our thoughts become things by the actions we take. It is the progress from those actions that make our dreams an eventual reality.

2
SHOW UP

- The first step in any endeavor is to show up! You cannot win a race if you don't run it.
- Punctuality is important, but it's equally important to be present and prepared, no matter how much work it takes.
- Go all in! Give your full and undivided time and attention to every task at hand.
- The desire and willingness to show up on good and bad days is what separates the successful from those who can't break through the barriers holding them back.

3
DON'T LISTEN TO YOUR WANTS AND DON'T WANTS

- Your "wants" and "don't wants" can get in the way of what you want to achieve. If you don't want to do something, you will procrastinate. If you want to hang out with friends, you're not likely to do the things you should do.
- With focus, commitment, and intentional effort, you can overcome your wants and don't wants and do what needs to be done.
- The more you control your thoughts and steer them in the direction you want them to go, the more they will work for you. The thoughts that dominate your beliefs and actions are the thoughts that will determine your results.

4
DISCIPLINE

- If your goal isn't worth the discipline to achieve it, it is nothing more than a wish.
- Discipline is a muscle that can be developed. It is a habit that can be strengthened and built.
- Do not let the thought of "work" get in your way, especially since work is the one thing that can bring you closer to your goals.
- Do the hardest thing first; the rest will then come easier.

5

DON'T WORRY ABOUT WHAT OTHERS THINK

- The only one you have to worry about is the person in the mirror. Focus on yourself, not others.
- You cannot control other people's actions or opinions. However, you can control your response to them.
- Worrying about the competition and what others are doing will only slow you down. Instead, turn your focus toward something productive. You'll find that you can't think about two things at the same time!

6

DON'T BE ATTACHED TO YOUR OUTCOMES

- It is always good to be committed to an outcome. It is rarely good to be emotionally attached to an outcome.
- Emotional attachment will have a negative effect on your judgment and actions.
- Being committed to an outcome keeps you in control of your thoughts. Attachment to an outcome lets your thoughts control your outcomes.

7
THE MINDSET OF SUCCESS

- Mindset constitutes 90 percent of what it takes to be successful.
- A strong mindset keeps you on track when fear, insecurities, and worries threaten to cloud your judgment.
- A weak or negative mindset will never produce positive results.
- What you focus on expands. Focus on good, and more good will come.
- Success is based on attitude, approach, and expectations.
- Strong body, strong mind.

8
DO THE RIGHT THING—ALWAYS

- No risk or amount of money is worth your integrity, which is the quality of being honest and having strong moral principles.
- Do the right things *always,* not just some of the time.
- When you do the right thing, there are no regrets, excuses, or negative consequences.

9

PAY ATTENTION

- Observation is an excellent instructor; pay attention to what people are saying and what they aren't saying.
- People will show you what they need and what their problems are if you pay attention.
- Your focus should not be solely on verbal or non-verbal communication. Focus on effective communication in whatever form it comes.

10

UNDER PROMISE AND OVER DELIVER

- Doing more than you say you will earns customer loyalty and referrals.
- When you over promise and under deliver, people are disappointed. The best way to create happy customers is to under promise, then exceed expectations.
- Set expectations, then set out to wow customers and clients.

11

HAVE FUN

- You only have one life—there are no dress rehearsals!
- Find joy and enjoyment at work and at play, in whatever you do.

- There is no need to sacrifice happiness and what brings you joy for you career—you can have both!

MORE DOMINANT THOUGHTS TO CONSIDER

Do we sanction incompetence in ourselves, or staff, or anyone around us?

Are we as skilled as we need to be to have an unfair advantage?

Are we in business with people that we shouldn't be, and what is the cost?

Are we consistently going after the top talent? If not, why not?

What are we doing on a daily basis to strengthen our mindset?

Eliminate the option called failure.

Remember, our ego will not only ruin our business, it will keep us from doing what we need to do.

Negative thinking is always more powerful than positive thinking; we have to eliminate it.

We must be unwavering in our desire, in spite of the daily ups and downs.

We must work daily to remove the drama around us.

Thinking big is a learned process.

Both our personal and business environments are critical to control to have a positive mindset.

What we focus on expands.

Discipline is critical for having and maintaining a strong mindset.

We are in the rejection business, the more we get rejected, the more business we will have.

We can build personal power by getting our thinking on track, our values in order, and our body in shape.

A major portion of our success is based upon these three words … attitude, approach, and expectations.

To create a stronger mindset, spend less time comparing yourself to others and more time trying to attain what is in your business plan.

Have a plan and work your plan – A goal without a plan is nothing more than a dream.

Be the best you can be – If I am going to do it, I'm going to give it my all—anything short of that never feels good.

Always focus on the two e's: efficiency and effectiveness – There are two ways to improve, by becoming more efficient and more effective. As a salesperson, efficiency was my systems and processes; my effectiveness was my skills and scripts.

Come with solutions, not problems—It is easy and commonplace to acknowledge the problems and then focus on them. The key is to focus on solutions.

Talent is key – When you hire, hire people who are as good or better than you at the role you are giving up or asking them to take over.

There is no substitute for talent; always hire the best and don't settle out of need.

The right "who" will enable you to achieve the "what" that you need to and will help you figure out the "how" to do it.

ABOUT CHRIS HELLER

Chris Heller, a native of Southern California, is a real estate industry icon and thought leader. Starting as an agent during his sophomore year in college, he has built one of the most successful real estate teams in the United States, from his selection as Rookie of the Year, to being the top-producing agent in San Diego County and ultimately the #1 Keller Williams associate in all of North America. Under Chris's leadership, the Heller Team has sold over 4,000 homes. Chris has succeeded in a highly competitive marketplace through his leadership, drive, and ability to assemble and empower high performing teams. Named President of KW Worldwide in 2010, Heller launched the company's first regions outside of North America, leading Keller Williams to record productivity and profitability. His vision and leadership helped grow the Company into the most dominant worldwide real estate franchise in history. In 2015, Heller was named CEO of KWRI, where he led the company to record growth and profits. He next became the CEO of mellohome, a sister company to LoanDepot, where he led cross-functional groups tasked with creating simpler and smarter home buying, financing, and improvement experiences for the American consumer. Under Heller's leadership, mellohome flourished, quickly {doubling} its forecasted growth and driving significant change within the experiential and product landscape for the homeownership industry at large.

Currently Chris is the Chief Real Estate Officer of OJO Labs, where he is shaping partner strategies, creating a cohesive structure and adoption between real estate professionals, consumers, and OJO. Chris Heller brings deep industry and leadership expertise, having held influential positions for more than 3 decades. Known internationally as an industry thought leader, advisor, and angel investor, Chris utilizes his extensive network for the benefit of his company and the others he advises and mentors. His four kids, Alli, Sophie, Nick, and Olivia, along with his wife, Nina, are the light of his life.

www.ChrisHeller.co

ABOUT GREG S. REID

For over 25 years, Greg has inspired millions of people to take personal responsibility to step into the potential of their greatness, and, as such, his life of contribution has been recognized by government leaders, a foreign Princess, as well as luminaries in education, business, and industry.

Mr. Reid has been published in over 120 books, including 32 bestsellers in 45 languages. Titles, such as *Stickability: The Power of Perseverance; The Millionaire Mentor,* and *Three Feet from Gold: Turn Your Obstacles into Opportunities,* have inspired countless readers to understand that the most valuable lessons we learn are also the easiest ones to apply.

Greg is known best for being the Founder of Secret Knock, a

Forbes and Inc. magazine top-rated event focused on partnership, networking, and business development.

He is the producer of the Oscar-qualified film, *Wish Man,* based on the creator of the Make A Wish Foundation.

For his work in mentoring youth in his hometown of San Diego, Mr. Reid was honored by the White House, where a former President commended Greg for positively working with youth through a local mentorship program.

And if that is not enough, recently Greg was honored with the star on the infamous Las Vegas Walk of Stars.

To learn more, visit Gregreid.com

Made in the USA
Columbia, SC
09 May 2022

60099582R00065